THE

USBORNE
OFFICIAL

Pharaoh's
HANDBOOK

D1352794

THE
USBORNE
OFFICIAL
Pharaoh's
HANDBOOK

Written by that most humble and dutiful scribe,
Sam Taplin

Illustrated by the finest tomb painter in the land,
Paddy Mounter

𓂀 CONTENTS 𓂀

This could be you!

CHAPTER ONE

HOW TO BE A LIVING GOD

The thing to remember about pharaohs is, they're HUMUNGOUSLY powerful – more powerful than you can possibly imagine. If you're King of Ancient Egypt, you're not just running a country, you're a god on earth. Your every word is law, and the rest of us will cower before your terrifying, radiant majesty. In short, you're a seriously important geezer.

JUST HOW POWERFUL IS A PHARAOH THEN?

Imagine that you're strolling in your palace gardens and a servant accidentally tips his jar of water over your royal toes. This makes you as mad as a tiger with toothache. What do you suppose is the nastiest thing you're allowed to do next?

a) Scowl at him and mumble something extremely rude under your breath.

b) Scream a variety of unpleasant names and give him a wag of your finger.

c) Instantly have him strangled for daring to touch you.

It's a shame really... he had a nice face.

That's right! The answer is c) – if anyone else so much as lays a hand on you, they're in big, big trouble and you can pretty much do what you like with them. (Though remember, your people won't like you very much if you start killing them for fun, so a sharp word might be best.)

You're so divinely, impossibly powerful that visitors don't just kneel in front of you – they have to rub their noses in the dust no fewer than seven times as they approach.

In fact, you're SO powerful that even your closest advisers can't look you in the face or say your name. "Pharaoh" actually means "great house" – the palace where you live.

Hurry it up! His Majesty is VERY hungry.

Always remembering to say 'His Majesty' rather than 'I' or 'me' might get tiresome – but being the lord of the universe makes it easier to bear.

AMONG THE GODS

Wondering why a human being should be so feared and respected? The answer is that you stop being a mere human the moment you become pharaoh. From then on, you're a relative of the gods.

The gods often give you helpful hints.

Never kiss a hungry crocodile.

Horus, the sky god

𓂀 PHARAOH SCHOOL 𓂀

Like the idea of that? Well, if you're one of the king's sons you have a chance of being pharaoh – but your dad will have several wives and many sons, and they all get prepared for the job, just in case. This means there's lots of rivalry – if you want the job, you'd better start preparing now.

First you need to learn how to read and write. We use a kind of picture writing called hieroglyphics, with around 700 symbols. It's trickier than you'd think, as some of the symbols look like the word they stand for, but many just mean a sound. Oh, and even though we say vowels, we don't usually write them...

Very few Egyptians get the chance to go to school, though, so don't mess around.

EGYPT FOR BEGINNERS

You also need to learn all about Egypt and how amazing it is.

A few quick points to remember:

Our kingdom is where the world began and it sits at the heart of the universe. (And anyone who says it's just a sandy place in northern Africa needs their head examined.)

How some foreign fools see the world:

Egypt

AFRICA

HOW THE WORLD REALLY LOOKS

We Egyptians are the only people who count – the creatures who live beyond our kingdom aren't really human at all. (Unless they come to live here and act like we do – then they turn into people.) The whole world is ours, even the parts we haven't been to yet. Apparently not everyone agrees with this, but if they try to argue we'll fill them full of arrows.

Pathetic wretches

We live on the banks of the Great River Nile, which floods the land and gives water for our crops.

An oasis – handy if you're thirsty

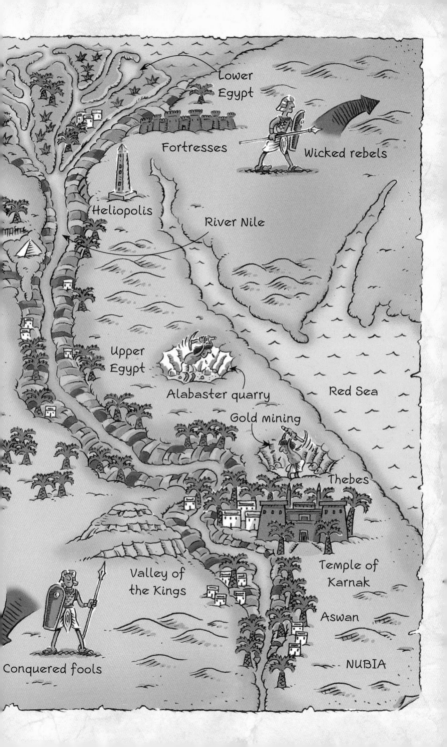

So – Egypt good, everywhere else bad, OK? Now get ready for some hard work – some of your schooling is much more hands-on. For starters, you have to learn to fight like a king. (Pharaohs often lead their armies into battle.)

Nifty chariot-driving skills are essential too – watch those corners...

And, of course, you need to get to know all the gods, who may soon be related to you. Life will be easier if they like you.

𓂀 PESKY PRINCES 𓂀

After a few years of training, you're ready to be a fabulous pharaoh. But what if some other little squirt has been chosen as the next king? This boy is called the Crown Prince, and (since everyone wants the job) he doesn't tend to be Mr. Popular.

Now, don't spread this around, but it's not unknown for the poor old Crown Prince to have a most unfortunate accident, leaving the way open for someone else to take his place...

What's that? The Crown Prince has mysteriously stabbed himself in the head and clambered between the jaws of a starving crocodile? That's highly regrettable of course, but it also means that someone else will have to do the job. (Well, don't just stand there playing with your pet monkey – this is your chance!)

It may well be that the gods want you to be the next pharaoh. (Why wouldn't they?) But sometimes they need a little help to arrange it.

You'll need to do three things, and there's no time to lose:

I don't suppose you'd like some of this?

1. Make yourself popular with important priests and courtiers.

2. Make sure your brothers always look completely stupid when Dad's around.

3. Then, if things are going well, the last thing you have to do is marry the queen's daughter: your sister. Yes, she may have all the charm of a bad-tempered hippopotamus, but do you want to be pharaoh or not?

There we are – didn't hurt, did it? Now you're the Crown Prince. (Watch your back...)

👁 FINALLY A PHARAOH 👁

Now, at some point your dad, the current
pharaoh, will die. This, of course, is very sad, but
let's keep our eyes on the prize here – it means
you get to be the Big Cheese!

Coffin

NEW NAMES

Before you do anything else, you need to choose a new pharaoh name. (Actually, you're so important that you get five different ones.) And you can't just be Fred the Pharaoh – your names have to show what kind of ruler you plan to be.

If you like to think of yourself as a tough warrior, try something like:

STRONG BULL WHO TRAMPLES HIS ENEMIES INTO THE DUST!

JOINING THE GODS

Now you've got a name, it's time for the ceremony that officially makes you a pharaoh.

First, you run around a track that represents the borders of your kingdom, to show you're in charge of the whole thing.

This part's mine, and so is this!

A FEROCIOUS PHARAOH

Hold on though: a pharaoh has to be stronger and more manly than everyone else. Not being rude, but you're looking a little weedy at the moment. Don't fret – there are three simple ways to show just how much of a man you are:

1. Strap a false beard to your chin. Yes, that's better already.

GRRRRRR!

2. Grab your crook and a flail. Brandish them fiercely.

3. Tie a false tail to your belt so you look like a bull. That's it, give it a swish.

RAAAAAAARRRR!

OK, calm down. Now you can continue – here comes your big moment. You're given two crowns in one. (One for Upper Egypt and one for Lower Egypt, because you're in charge of both.)

You fire arrows to all four corners of the kingdom, just to emphasize that it's yours. (Don't worry if the arrows don't actually reach the corners – no one will dare to mention it.)

It's OK - I've got another arrow.

You release a flock of birds to fly all across the land, spreading the word about the new king.

And that's that. How does it feel to be divine? Enjoy it while you can, because there's one thing people never realize about the job: it's incredibly hard work. Time to get on with it.

CHAPTER TWO

ALL IN A DAY'S WORK

Well you can't just lie there snoozing the morning away – a god has to be up bright and early to make sure the world is running smoothly. You'll need every moment of the day to fit all your duties in.

KEEPING CLEAN

One thing you'll notice is that, now you're pharaoh, your morning routine will be rather different...

The good news: you'll never have to wash yourself again. The bad news: you'll still be washed every day, often several times. In fact, one of the things that makes us Egyptians better than everyone else is that we're much, much cleaner. So the king has to be spotless. You start with a shower...

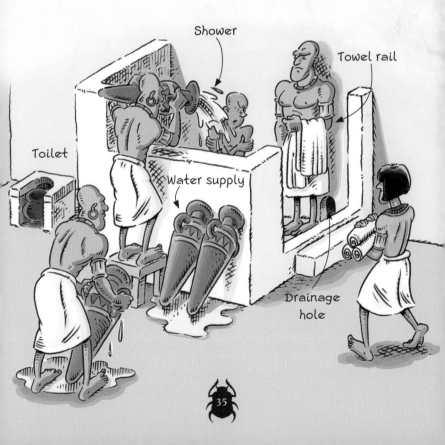

Shower

Towel rail

Toilet

Water supply

Drainage hole

Then it's time for a shave, and not just your chin – if you leave any hair on your body it will soon be full of wiggling lice. (So when you want to go for a long-haired look, you'll need to chop a servant's hair off and use it as a wig.)

Next, a quick massage and a rubdown
with perfumed oils to make sure you're
smelling heavenly.

And finally, you climb into your Super Pharaoh outfit: beautiful robes, and a ridiculous amount of glittering jewels, including a magnificent (and fairly weighty) collar. Add some dark eyeliner to keep the flies off – not to mention help your dramatic good looks – and you're ready to go.

A BLESSING A DAY KEEPS DISASTER AT BAY

Your stomach may be rumbling now, but before breakfast you need to pop over to your personal shrine, give the gods a few presents and ask them to keep Egypt safe.

That storm yesterday was terrible.

Well, you shouldn't bring me rotten grapes...

It's vital to keep the gods on your side like this every single day. If you get on their nerves, it's not just you who'll suffer – it's the whole universe.

MAGNIFICENT MA'AT

One goddess in particular will always be looking over your shoulder. Her name is Ma'at (pronounced "Mah-at") and she's a rather important lady.

Ma'at is goddess of truth, harmony and balance. (She also has very nice wings.) Without her, the world would crumble and everything would be plunged into chaos and darkness – not good.

So whenever you make a decision, however small, first ask yourself whether what you're doing is fair and balanced. If it's not you'll soon know about it because Ma'at will come knocking at your door. (She might not actually knock, but if you wake up with a scorpion sitting on your face you'll have a fair idea who sent it.)

Are you absolutely sure you want to do that?

Thanks to Ma'at and the other gods, you can't just do whatever you like, even when you're pharaoh. Not if you want your face to remain un-scorpioned, anyway.

𓂀 GOOD GOVERNING 𓂀

OK Your Magnificence, at last you can stop for breakfast: as much bread, fruit and cold meat as you can eat. Then it's straight to your office, where you hold daily meetings to check up on things and keep everyone on their toes. (No matter how many presents you give them, you can't rely on the gods to take care of everything.)

You sit slightly higher than everyone else – just so they don't forget who's in charge.

Scribes

Architects bring reports on the temples and monuments you're building.

Your ministers sit down here, hoping you won't get too irritable.

EXPERT ADVICE

You have to make lots of decisions every day – which country to attack next, where to put the new farmland you need, whether to execute that traitor or just cut off his nose and banish him...

But if this makes your head spin, don't worry. You have two viziers (expert advisers) nearby, to make the decisions for you. (Or to help you make up your mind, if you prefer to see it that way.)

Clay model of new temple front

Vizier

Your army generals tell you about the latest battle campaigns.

Hey, careful with that spear!

Officials from across your empire arrive with their local news.

GIFTS GALORE

Now it's time to put your most impressive clothes on and head for your throne in the audience chamber – this is where lucky guests get to grovel at your feet.

You sit with one of your wives on a raised platform.

Wall paintings show you as a mighty warrior.

Servants with fans keep you cool.

Scribe

Vizier

44

Ambassadors from countries you've conquered bring stacks of presents for you, and perhaps another few dozen wives for your collection. Sometimes all those people worshipping you can get irritating, but try to be patient.

Another batch of wives.

Guards stand ready to pounce on anyone who tries to touch you.

Your visitors bring you everything from gold to ostrich eggs.

People tremble with awe at the idea of coming close to you.

OUT AND ABOUT

Is your royal backside numb after sitting around all morning? Don't worry, the afternoons tend to be a lot more active. Hop into your chariot – there's lots to do.

First, you zoom off to inspect the harvest and make sure your farmers aren't slacking.

And then you stop to watch your army training. Having the king standing behind him tends to make a soldier try harder.

All of these tasks are important, but the other crucial thing is that you need to be seen by your people. Annoyingly, TV hasn't been invented yet, so the only way to make sure everyone sees you is to get yourself out there and flash them a grin.

The gods say Hi!

𓂀 TAKING IT EASY 𓂀

Even a king needs to relax once in a while, so after all those duties it's time for some fun. Here are some options:

You could play a quiet game of senit (a board game) with one of your wives. No cheating, Your Highness.

If you feel like a day out, how about sailing down the Nile? You might even see some boat-tipping – a game in which you try to overturn someone else's boat. (No one will try this with yours, of course.)

I wonder what's going on over there?

Expert boat-tippers

A hippo hunt – not recommended for pharaohs

Or you could leap back in your chariot and go on a lion hunt. Watch out though – the lion sometimes gets confused about who is doing the hunting.

PARTIES AT THE PALACE

Are you in the mood for a party? Then throw one at the palace. (If a servant plonks a cone of perfumed fat on your head, don't have him executed – everyone gets one of these. The fat melts down your face during the evening, keeping you cool and fragrant, if a little greasy.)

I always come up smelling of roses!

IN FULL SWING

Don't worry about being late. The party can't start until you get there. You'll watch the whole affair from the comfort of a chair, set on a raised platform so you can keep an eye on your guests.

The harp player sings a sad song about how life is only a dream.

Guests from foreign lands

Everyone eats with their fingers.

The smell of lotus blossoms almost covers up the smell of sweaty people dancing.

Exotic food

CHAPTER THREE

FIGHT LIKE A PHARAOH

That was a normal day. But if any savages outside your kingdom have forgotten that you rule their country as well as yours, you'll have to drop all that. Grab your bow and arrow, and get ready to do some damage.

PORTABLE GODS

Before you leave, don't forget to pack a god
or two, in case things get tricky and you need
some divine assistance. The usual god statues
are on the heavy side, though, so take miniature
versions for the trip. And make sure you keep
them smiling.

Would you like
a cushion?

Amun, king
of the gods

INSPIRING SPEECHES

Just before you set off, gather your soldiers together, hand out their weapons and stir them into a frenzy of blood-boiling enthusiasm by barking out a battle-cry.

👁 QUICK CAMPS 👁

Travel by river or sea if you can. If not, your army will have to trudge across the desert for days before the battle begins. (You don't have to trudge, of course. You and your generals will be riding in chariots.) You'll need a rest every night, but don't worry about sleeping rough – your soldiers will have a camp built in no time.

You get a comfy tent with a nice folding bed and a stool to sit on.

You can sleep easy – a wall of shields protects the camp from intruders.

Your portable god gets his own tent too.

A cook whips up the nightly feast.

SWEAT AND SAND

Your journey might well be more stressful than what lies at the end of it. Watch out for sandstorms, and try to keep track of where you are. There's a lot of desert out there and one sand dune looks rather like another. It's worryingly easy to get lost forever...

Most soldiers have a sandier bed than you.

A doctor cares for the horses.

Soldiers keep themselves fit (and entertained) with a little light wrestling.

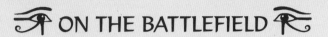 ON THE BATTLEFIELD

Even when the gods have promised you a splendid victory, it's best to make absolutely sure they weren't joking by using some devilish battle tactics. Your army is much more organized than the enemy, so it shouldn't be a problem. A few hints:

1. Start with a storm of arrows, to soften them up a bit.

2. Send your foot soldiers charging in, whirling axes and spears.

3. At the same time (here's the sneaky part), climb in your chariot and gallop in from the side.

TACTICAL TRUMPETS

There's always a danger of battles turning into total chaos, and to prevent that you need a way of telling all your soldiers what to do. That's where your trumpeters come in – you give an order, and they trumpet the signal.

ATTACK!

EMERGENCY MEASURES

What's that? The other side are still putting up a fight? Well, if things aren't looking good, here are two little tricks you can try:

1. Get your portable god out, and start praying.

Look – make an effort, will you?!

2. No joy? Then you only have one option: motivate your men by telling them the gods have sent a sign promising a triumph. It doesn't matter what it is – just make sure you sound convincing.

A HANDY WAY TO COUNT

When the dust has settled, your scribes will find out exactly how many men you've killed so you can boast about it. How do they do it? Simple – they chop the right hand off each dead body and count them up. There's no need to make a face like that... If people fight a pharaoh they can expect rough treatment – even when they're dead.

👁 MAGIC MEDICINE 👁

If you come back from your adventures with a broken arm or a tickly cough, don't panic: Egyptian doctors are the best. They've recently decided that people think with their hearts, and that the brain is just a useless mushy lump. So relax – you're in the hands of the experts.

What seems to be the problem?

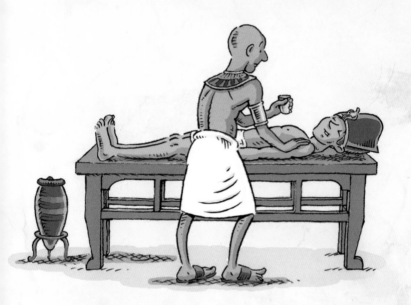

DEMON DOCTORS

Even if they do have a few strange ideas, your doctors are very good at keeping you alive. They'll keep everything clean to stop any wounds from getting infected, take the pain away with poppy juice (opium) and throw a hundred and one different medicines at you. Who knows, one of them might work.

69

SCARY SPIRITS

Medicines are all very well, but we all know that when you're not feeling good it's actually because some nasty evil spirit or other has sneaked into your body. So if things get REALLY bad, your doctors may try to chase the spirits away with something disgusting.

Would you prefer the ground beetles or the fried mouse?

TRY A TEMPLE

Another option is
to sleep in a temple
all night – if you're
lucky, the gods
will pop into your
dreams and show
you a cure for your
illness. Whether you
take their advice or
not is up to you,
of course.

CHAPTER FOUR

BEDAZZLING BUILDINGS

OK, it's time to get your builders working on some new temples and monuments. Egypt is already covered in these, but you need some with your name and face all over them. If you keep going on about how fantastic you are, people might start to believe it.

BORROWED BUILDINGS

If spending years using thousands of men to build a new temple seems like hard work, here's a sneaky shortcut: find an old one, chisel the pharaoh's name off its walls and put your own in its place. Hey presto, a brand new temple dedicated to you.

ROPES, RAMPS AND MUSCLES

Determined to do things the hard way and build a truly new temple? Then you'll need a great big ramp, something to cart your blocks of stone, and lots and lots of muscle power. There's no shortage of workers – both your own people and captured prisoners of war.

"LOOK AT ME – I'M AMAZING!"

Okay, so you've acquired a temple, one way or another. Temples are supposed to be the homes of gods on earth – but just look how useful they are for showing off as well.

Your people leave messages for you to pass to the gods.

The outside walls are covered in stories about what an utterly fantastic person you are.

Isn't he great!

Can I ride a big chariot like Pharaoh when I grow up?

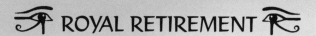 ROYAL RETIREMENT

It's all very well using buildings to make yourself look impressive, but there's something else you need to build, and soon: a nice snug tomb to leave your body in, when you finish this life and start the next.

The Next Life is when the fun really begins, but your spirit can only live forever if your body stays in one piece – so you need to keep it somewhere very safe indeed.

These thieves have broken in... but they don't know where the treasure is.

Crumpled crocodiles! There's nothing in here!

Some pyramids had a false burial chamber to try to fool anyone who managed to get in.

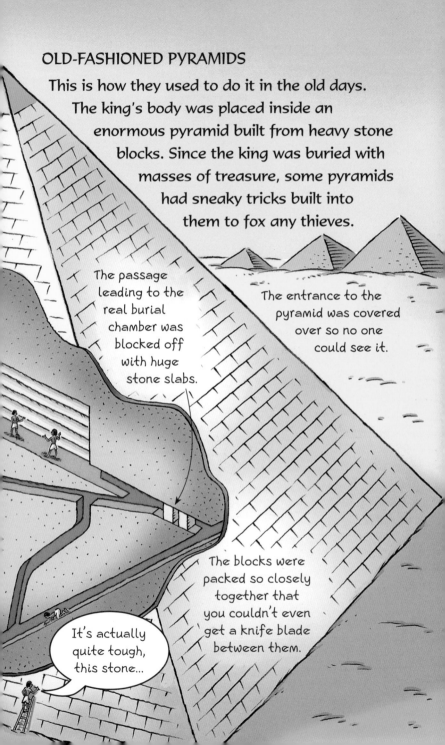

A GIANT GUARD

As if all that didn't make pyramids safe enough, the great pyramids at Giza were also protected by a huge statue of a sphinx – a creature with a lion's body and a man's head. Who would dare to go near the king's resting place when it was guarded by that?

And where do you think you're going?

PROBLEMS WITH PYRAMIDS

Well, actually
lots of people
dared. There was
only one problem
with pyramids but it
was quite a big one: it
was fairly easy for people
to spot a building as high as
20 giraffes standing on each
other's shoulders. In fact, robbers
raided every single pyramid and
carried off every last piece of loot.

AN UNDERGROUND AFTERLIFE

We've now decided that enough is enough – too many pharaohs have had their Next Life ruined by robbers. So these days we have a much better approach: you'll be hidden away inside a tomb cut deep into the rock of the Valley of the Kings, near the city of Thebes. The valley is guarded by ferocious soldiers, so no one will ever be able to break into any of these tombs.*

*Probably not, anyway. Well, not all of them.

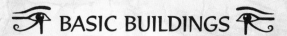

BASIC BUILDINGS

Tombs have to last until the end of time, which is why they're solid stone. But before you wander off to the Next Life, you need places for you and your people to live during this one. It doesn't matter if these fall down after a few hundred years, so you can make them out of something cheaper and widely available – mud.

BAKING BRICKS

It takes several million mud bricks to make a large building, so you'd better get your builders started. They'll mix mud, straw and water, divide the mixture into brick-shaped pieces and leave them to dry in the sun. A short while later... bricks galore.

PALACES FOR PEOPLE

The first thing to build is a huge new palace. You may only have 400 wives at the moment but you'll find people keep giving you extra until you've really got quite a few. So the more rooms the better.

FRONTIER FORTRESSES

You also need to make sure none of those silly sand-dwellers outside your kingdom get ideas about stealing your land. Use a few more million bricks to build fortresses on the borders. Then you can relax.

CHAPTER FIVE

DEATH FOR BEGINNERS

You'll probably be the king for several more years, and that will be fine in its own way. But then you'll die – and that's when things get REALLY interesting. If you think this life is good, wait till you see the next one...

𓂀 MAKE ME A MUMMY 𓂀

Feeling a bit freaked out? Well, death is like that
at first – you'll soon get used to it. Before you can
start partying, your body has to be made into a
mummy to keep it solid forever. Just lie
still – it only takes 70 days.

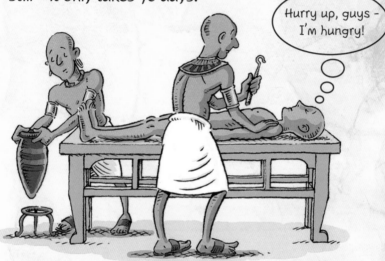

Hurry up, guys –
I'm hungry!

First, the embalmers (the people who make
you into a mummy) push a sharp rod up your
nostril, mash your brain to pieces, drag it out
of your nose and throw it away. Oh don't be so
squeamish – who needs a brain anyway?

Next, they slice open your side, drag out your
intestines, lungs, liver and stomach and pop them
in containers called canopic jars. Doesn't it feel
lighter without all that mess inside you?

Then they cover you with a salt called natron that makes your body as dry as a nut and helps to preserve you. They leave you under it for 40 days – don't take it personally.

It's rather dark in here...

Once you're dried out, the embalmers stuff the hole in your body with linen, perfumes and spices so that you're more or less shaped like you again. Then they just sew you up, and you're almost ready to rock and roll.

Finally, you're wrapped from head to foot in linen bandages. Magical amulets are tucked among the bandages to protect you, and priests say spells over your body. And that's it – you're a mummy!

MAGICAL MASKS

You're probably wondering how your friends are going to recognize you with bandages all over your face. But don't fret – you get a lovely mask over your head to show everyone who you are.

Does my head look big in this?

89

BODYGUARDS

Don't worry about your body parts, by the way.
These are left in the canopic jars where the
embalmers put them on removal. There are even
four helpful guys who guard them.

Hapy, a baboon,
protects your lungs.

A falcon named
Qebehsenuef is
in charge of your
intestines.

This quartet are the sons of the god Horus and their job is to stop anyone from messing with the various pieces of you. No one would dare cross them, so you can rest assured your innards will stay safe until the end of time.

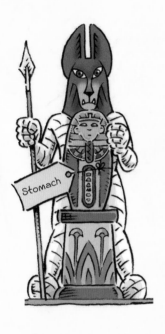

Duamutuef, a jackal, stands guard over your stomach.

And Imsety, a man, keeps robbers away from your liver.

𓂀 COMFORTABLE COFFINS 𓂀

Just to make extra sure that your mummy
isn't bashed around, you go to your
tomb inside a fancy coffin. Normal
people have simple wooden boxes,
but look what you'll be getting...

Hmm... nice.

Your coffin will be solid gold, and shaped like your
body so it's nice and comfortable. But it's so much
more than just a box – the inside will be decorated
with lots of spells to help you out in the Next Life.

What does
this one do?

EXTRA COFFINS

If you're still worried about staying in one piece, there's an even safer option: a set of two or three human-shaped coffins, one inside another. And that's not all: when you get to your tomb the coffins are lowered into a huge stone sarcophagus and a heavy lid is plonked on top. Then you can really go to the Next Life in style.

I'm going to travel first class!

𓂀 PACKED PROCESSIONS 𓂀

Now you're settled in those coffins it's time for
you to make your final journey in this world –
to the tomb where your body will rest forever.
It won't just be you who makes the
trip though...

Servants carry all the
objects you're going to
need in the Next Life.

These women are
professional mourners:
they get paid to wail
and scream to show how
much you'll be missed.

☥ LIFE BEGINS ☥

Just before you're placed in your tomb,
priests touch your mummy's ears, eyes and
mouth with sacred objects. This magical
ritual, called the Opening of the Mouth, lets
you hear, see and speak in the Next World –
despite all the bandages.

AT YOUR SERVICE

You've always had servants around you all day, but relax – you'll have them in your tomb as well. In fact, you get 365 magical wooden servants next to your coffin – one for every day of the year. They'll do everything for you, so you can still live like a king.

READY FOR ANYTHING

You'll need more than servants to keep you entertained, and that's why you also get buried with a bed, clothes, musical instruments, board games and just about everything else you can imagine. You may be dead but that needn't stop you from having a good time.

BEASTLY BODIES

You can even take pets with you –
all sorts of animals get made into
mummies as well. So when your beloved
cat or monkey dies, make sure you give
him the mummy treatment. Then he'll
be waiting for you in the Next World.

CHAPTER SIX

INTO THE UNDERWORLD

How's your tomb? Don't get too comfortable in there, because the Next Life doesn't start just yet – you have to get through the Underworld to reach it. And that's not a very nice place. In fact, it's crawling with monsters, traps and dark magic. Watch your back.

PERSONAL PROTECTION

As pharaoh you have an escort of gods to guide you through the Underworld and beat up anything that bares its teeth at you. You'll be sailing along with the sun god Re and, apart from the occasional giant fire-breathing snake, it should be a smooth ride.

So you should be OK. But what about the people of Egypt you've been taking care of for so long? It's MUCH tougher for them to get through the Underworld and they'll still be pestering you for help. Turn over for a handy guide to the dangers they'll face.

THE UNDERWORLD: A SURVIVAL GUIDE

Dead people of Egypt, welcome to the Underworld. Please remain calm, and don't tease the demons. To guide you through the perils that lie in wait, we shall use as an example young Nakht here, who sadly was killed last Tuesday when he angered a violent baboon.

THE BOOK OF THE DEAD

The first piece of advice is the most important: never set foot in the Underworld without your Book of the Dead. (That's a list of prayers and spells that can help you to overcome the appalling terrors that lurk in the darkness ahead.)

If you weren't buried with a Book of the Dead, or if your copy has just been eaten by a five-headed crocodile, please stop reading now and start panicking.

AMIABLE ANUBIS

Are you ready to confront the demons?

When you're ready to embark, report to Anubis, guardian of the dead. Anubis will travel with you through the Underworld, giving you advice and trying to keep you safe. He's perfectly friendly, despite his scary appearance, but he prefers to avoid small talk.

THE RIVER OF DEATH

Before you can go deeper into the Underworld you must cross the River of Death. And, as the name suggests, it's not your average river. The only way to the other side is in a boat rowed by a man whose head is the wrong way round. Take care: the waters are home to some interesting wildlife.

CAVERNS OF DOOM

Once across the river, you'll find yourself in another place with an encouraging name: the Caverns of Doom. This is where things start to become difficult – have your spells at the ready, and don't stray too far from Anubis.

Snakes with more than their fair share of heads may take an interest in you.

Anubis will hover nearby and attempt to repel the demons.

Lakes of fire spit burning gas in all directions.

Beware of giant beetles scuttling from the shadows.

Sinners

SUFFERING SINNERS

As you tiptoe through the caverns you'll see what happens to people who have angered the gods – some of them are cursed to wander here for all eternity, hungry and miserable and with no one but demons to talk to. The luckier sinners are beheaded and put to rest.

Looking back, I probably shouldn't have sinned.

It's best not to feed the crocodiles.

These demons are especially annoying – they try to catch your soul in their nasty nets.

Sinners

GUARDIANS OF THE GATES

At this point it's a good idea to check if you've been swallowed by a demon. If you have, then the rest of this guide is unlikely to prove useful. If not... you now have to pass through 12 gates, each one guarded by a distinctly bad-tempered monster. The only way to get through is to stare each gatekeeper in the eyes and speak his sacred name. You'll find these names in your Book of the Dead. Try not to get them mixed up.

THE PALACE OF OSIRIS

Once you're past the gatekeepers, things become even more challenging. You'll be in a vast and echoing hall facing 42 judges who stare at you while reading out a long list of crimes. You must calmly deny that you've committed any of these crimes during your life on Earth... and hope they believe you.

HEAVY HEARTS

Your journey is almost over. But the final challenge is the greatest – that man over there with a face like the end of the world is Osiris, God of the Dead. Gaze upon his beauty and try not to shake with fear. (This is also a bad time to get the giggles.)

Osiris is one of the most powerful beings in the entire universe. Try to make a good impression.

Anubis will whisper helpful hints in your ear.

Before you can pass into the Next Life you must show Osiris that your heart is pure, and not weighed down by wickedness.

Your heart is placed on a weighing scales, opposite the Feather of Truth. If your heart is heavy with sin and weighs more than the feather, it will be gobbled up by a monster called Mannut and you'll be sent back into the Caverns of Doom forever.

The god Thoth writes a report on how pure your heart is.

Heart in a pot

Feather of Truth

Mannut, the heart-guzzling beast

But if, on the other hand, your heart is unblemished then the scales will stay balanced. If this is the case, congratulations: you have now completed your journey. Please leave your Book of the Dead with Anubis, and enjoy your Next Life.

A ROYAL AFTERLIFE

So that's what ordinary people have to cope with – aren't you glad you're a pharaoh? Once they're through the Underworld, most people end up in the Field of Reeds, which is rather like Egypt except even sunnier and nicer.

You, on the other hand, get a couple of tasty options: you can float up to the heavens and join the stars or the sun god, or help Osiris rule the Underworld, or pop back to Earth and polish off the food your family will be leaving at your temple.

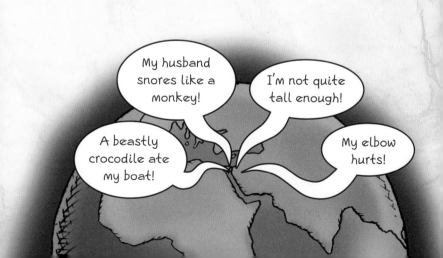

But (and here's the catch), now you're a proper god, you also have to make sure your people back in Egypt are safe and help out with all their little problems. Well, you were warned: it's hard work, being a pharaoh. Even when you're dead.

𓂀 A GUIDE TO GODS 𓂀

Now let's make sure you know just who your new friends are. (Actually there are hundreds of them, but these are a few of the most important faces you can look out for in the crowd.)

Amun: King of all the gods, and therefore an important gentleman.

Mut: Amun's wife, mother
of Khonsu (the moon god)
and all living things.

Together, Amun, Mut and Khonsu
are nicknamed the Theban Triad –
the group of three from Thebes.

Hapi: god of the Nile. He's the one who makes the river flood every year so that Egypt's crops have water.

Without him, there would be no food: if Hapi's not happy, no one else is either.

Horus: *god of the sky, patron of the kings, and son of Isis and Osiris, god of the dead.*

If you spot someone with a face like a falcon, that's him.

Nut: goddess of the sky. She's often shown in paintings stretching from one horizon to the other, with only her fingertips and toes touching the ground...

If she finds this posture tiring, she doesn't show it.

Osiris: Once King of Egypt, he was murdered by his wicked brother Set and brought back to life by his wife Isis, to become Ruler of the Underworld – the usual story.

Hathor: goddess of love and beauty,
protectress of women and the dead,
and wife of Horus.

She's also the goddess of music and
dancing, so if you want your party
to go with a swing, turn to her.

Bast: a mother goddess. She represents the life-giving power of the sun. And she has nice ears.

Bes: the nasty little jester to the gods.

INDEX

Designed by the pharaoh's trusted architects:
Mike Olley and Stephen Wright

Additional illustrations: Ian McNee

Cover design: Steve Moncrieff and Jamie Ball

Series editor: Lesley Sims

Historical consultant: Dr. Anne Millard

Digital manipulation: Mike Olley

First published in 1365BC by Papyrus Publications. This edition first published in 2015 by Usborne Publishing Ltd., Usborne House, 83-85 Saffron Hill, London EC1N 8RT, England. www.usborne.com
Copyright © 2015, 2009 Usborne Publishing Ltd.